How to Memorize All the U.S. Presidents and Anything Else You Need to Remember

Dr. Johnny Frog

Illustrations and composition
Thierry Martinet

Eloquent Books
New York, New York

Eloquent Books
An imprint of Strategic Book Group
P.O. Box 333
Durham CT 06422
www.StrategicBookGroup.com

ISBN: 978-1-60911-119-9

Printed in the United States of America

Book Design: Rolando F. Santos

To my wife Vesna and my six children:
Chloé, Maxime, Edouard, Amélie, Nicolas, and Charlie.
Thanks for your patience towards your husband and daddy.

Contents

Preface

Le Journal du Dimanche is a Sunday French newspaper. One Sunday as I was scanning the articles, a picture of France's new leader, President Nicolas Sarkozy, caught my eye. He was sitting regally in between the two Bush men. I don't mean the ones wielding axes at pine trees, either. Number forty-one was on one side and number forty-three was on the other side, each with individual numbers clearly and proudly embossed on their jackets.

The numbers forty-one and forty-three, of course, represent their respective standings as occupants of the White House. George Bush, Sr. was the forty-first president and George Bush, Jr., was the forty-third president. I never thought of the American presidents in terms of numbers before this moment, but it dawned on me that I didn't know the presidents by their numerical history or in exact order. Out of curiosity, I sought the help of my American friends. After long conversations on this topic, I recognized that very few of my friends could name all forty-four presidents in chronological order, and none of them could do it without mixing a few of them up. It's here that my project began with a proven method of knowing—not simply memorizing—but really knowing all forty-four American presidents. The method took shape, was proven, and I now am happy to share with you the how-to in this easy-to-follow guide.

In less time than you can imagine, you will know all forty-four presidents and their rankings in the White House. I will reveal, as a magician reveals his secrets, my simple method in this easy-to-follow instruction book.

To toot my own horn, I know all forty-four American presidents by name and number in any order, and by any ranking. This astounded my American friends. The entire process took me less than a few hours of amusing word and image associations to remember them all. I also use this method in business with incredible results.

After reading this book, you too will be able to understand and apply my method to any subject matter, such as remembering all of America's first ladies, the American states, the European countries, the capitals of the world, and along with the world leaders.

──────── **The photo that started it all** ────────

"En balade avec les Bush"

Nicolas Sarkozy boating with Presidents 41 and 43 at Kennebunkport.

(photo: Jim Watson /AFP)

If you are a student, you will ace exams. If you are an executive, you will remember important information critical for business meetings, managing teams, or running an entire organization. Or, if you're like me and you're curious about the world around you, then you will be able to discover and recall the endless amount of information it holds. The possibilities are as large as your desire to learn

Like any board game, you have to understand the rules before you play—this is no different. Start slowly and methodically, have a few sheets of paper and a pencil handy. Marvel at the vast amounts of information you will start to accumulate in your memory without breaking a sweat.

Let the game begin...

What you can expect to see in this book

The sea horse is what I call a brain jogger. This box will jog your memory on the important basics throughout the book so you don't have to keep flipping back and forth.

Use the brain jogger liberally, and eventually you will stop looking at it and needing it to move forward.

All extra information, whether it is contained in this book or you reference it elsewhere, can be added to the basic rule. It will allow you to build a skyscraper of information on any given topic and make your knowledge easily accessible and, most importantly, your memory stronger.

Like anything, there are the basics. Here the basic rules are so simple and easy to remember that even a teenager can do it.

First, remember the formula. You will find it under the sea horse throughout the book to help you remember.

To begin, we will start with the formatting of forty-four boxes directly into a specific region of your brain called the hippocampus. This will allow you to track the chronology.

The next step is to load different associations in order to bridge the gap between the left and right hemispheres of your brain.

You will learn how to unleash your memory and reach levels that will simply amaze you.

You will find yourself daring anyone and everyone to test your knowledge.

You won't be able to resist!

A basic introduction
to your memory

Any event, whether it be remarkable or not, such as a wedding, a funeral, meeting someone new, the education we receive along the way—anything that can be seen or heard—is information for your brain to decide whether it should be saved.

If your brain thinks the information is worthy, it saves it in your memory bank; if not, it's gone like the wind.

As you probably know, your brain has different parts (Fig. 1)

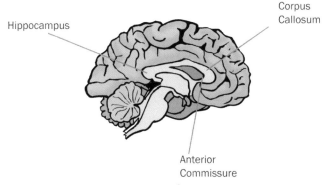

Hippocampus

Corpus Callosum

Anterior Commissure

Fig.1 Anatomy of your brain

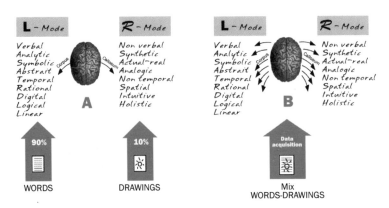

Fig.2: Modes of data acquisition

Some of these parts are important for what we recall or remember.

The hippocampus is one of the more important parts of the brain. It processes memories that contain old and new information, or memories that are being processed and stored away in the different areas of the cerebral cortex, or the gray matter of the brain. This is the largest, outermost part of the brain.

Figure 2, Mode A shows the left hemisphere processes the verbal and analytical thinking data, and the right hemisphere processes the visual and perceptual thinking data.

Our purpose in this book is not to perpetuate another brain scam discussion on whether someone is more left-brained or right-brained, but to show you that we are both.

Like many things in life, such as yin and yang or black and white, we need to manage duality.

Let's say (for discussion purposes) that the other popular brain scam is that we use only ten percent of our brain's capacity. Wrong!

We live in an environment where we do what we do, we are who we are, communicating and co-existing, while using words for an astonishing ninety percent of that communication. Some communications studies state that non-verbal communication is sixty percent of how we communicate.

When we have to memorize something, we use the left part of our brain. If we change the environment, then we use the right part. The percentage will change immensely. This will result in changing how you will remember, process, and ultimately use the data.

It's quite simple: when you remember something, you tend to act on it or use it. When you don't remember something, you don't act on it.

Thanks to the corpus callosum, you will be able to build a free-flowing freeway from one side to another and end up with a synergetic outcome—a balance.

The aim of this book is to encourage you to use both sides of your brain (maybe not equally, but certainly more freely) instead of using only the left side as you were trained to do your entire life (Fig. 2 Mode B).

Most problems we encounter, however, are because the left brain is dominant and speedy and prone to vigorously processing data. We will show you how to take a piece of data, turn it down with the dominant left side, using only the parts of the left brain you need, while introducing the right side into the equation.

For example, you could very well learn the following list of forty-four presidents as any good left-brainer—by heart. This could be considered a boring task and certainly not an entertaining one.

Contained below you will find the full list of forty-four presidencies. The number on the left indicates the consecutive time in office served by a single person. For example, George Washington served two consecutive terms and is counted as the first president, not the first and the second president. Gerald Ford assumed the presidency after the resignation of Richard Nixon, serving out the remainder of what would have been Nixon's second term. The fact that Ford was not voted into office does not affect the numbering, which makes him the thirty-eighth president. Grover Cleveland served two non-consecutive terms and is therefore counted chronologically as both the twenty-second and the twenty-fourth president. Because of this, the list actually contains forty-four presidencies, but only forty-three presidents.

Depending on your level of training and your experience to manage long laundry lists, you will be able to learn this list by heart without the method we propose. It will probably take several booster shoots before you may be ultimately successful, but you could do it, of course. You will know it, be able to recite it, but definitively not remember it forever. Maybe you think that is acceptable for exam purposes, but what a shame not to learn it and remember it forever so you can pull out the information somewhere down the line. This is the same problem everyone is facing in our current education system here in the U.S. or abroad. You are taught and learn massive amounts of information by linear method.

Let's change that by starting here. Take a look at the list of presidents and their terms in office, along with the dates they served:

1 - George Washington, 1789-1797, two terms
2 - John Adams, 1797-1801, one term
3 - Thomas Jefferson, 1801-1809, two terms
4 - James Madison, 1809-1817, two terms
5 - James Monroe, 1817-1825, two terms
6 - John Quincy Adams, 1825-1829, one term
7 - Andrew Jackson, 1829-1837, two terms
8 - Martin Van Buren, 1837-1841, one term
9 - William H. Harrison, 1841 (died in office)
10 - John Tyler, 1841-1845, one term
11 - James K. Polk, 1845-1849, one term
12 - Zachary Taylor, 1849-1850
13 - Millard Fillmore, 1850-1853, one term
14 - Franklin Pierce, 1853-1857, one term
15 - James Buchanan, 1857-1861, one term
16 - Abraham Lincoln, 1861-1865, one term
17 - Andrew Johnson, 1865-1869, one term
18 - Ulysses S. Grant, 1869-1877, two terms
19 - Rutherford B Hayes, 1877-1881, one term
20 - James Garfield, 1881 (died in office)
21 - Chester A. Arthur, 1881-1885, one term
22 - Grover Cleveland, 1885-1889, one term
23 - Benjamin Harrison, 1889-1893, one term
24 - Grover Cleveland, 1893-1897, one term
25 - William McKinley, 1897-1901, one term
26 - Theodore Roosevelt, 1901-1909, two terms
27 - William H. Taft, 1909-1913, one term
28 - Woodrow Wilson, 1913-1921, two terms
29 - Warren G. Harding, 1921-1923, one term
30 - Calvin Coolidge, 1923-1929, one term

31 - Herbert Hoover, 1929-1933, one term
32 - Franklin D. Roosevelt, 1933-1945, three terms
33 - Harry S. Truman, 1945-1953, two terms
34 - Dwight D. Eisenhower, 1953-1961, two terms
35 - John F. Kennedy, 1961-1963, one term
36 - Lyndon B. Johnson, 1963-1969, one term
37 - Richard Nixon, 1969-1974, one term
38 - Gerald Ford, 1974-1977, one term
39 - Jimmy Carter, 1977-1981, one term
40 - Ronald Reagan, 1981-1989, two terms
41 - George H. W. Bush, 1989-1993, one term
42 - Bill Clinton, 1993-2001, two terms
43 - George W. Bush, 2001-2008, two terms
44 - Barack Obama, 2009

Chapter 1

Build your own boxes in your hippocampus

Instead of writing words or phrases repetitively to remember data, we will use a mixture of drawings, words, letters, and figures and draw them only once. This method is a new way to memorize data. In fact, by doing this you will use your brain in a different way.

Later on you will be required to build your own boxes in your hippocampus—a sort of storage space system where you will be able to put your word associations and access them at random.

The human brain has about one hundred billion neurons. With an estimated average of one thousand

1

connections between each neuron and its neighbours, we have about 100 trillion connections, with each one capable of simultaneous calculations. Phew! That's one amazing parallel processing tool and an essential key to the strength of human thinking and the way the mind works.

A profound weakness, however, is the slow speed of neural circuitry—only 200 calculations per second. For problems that involve massive parallelism, such as neural net-based pattern recognition, the human brain does a great job. However, for problems that require extensive sequential thinking, the human brain is mediocre.

The right mode is postulated to be a mode of massive parallel processing, and the left mode is purposed to be a sequential processing mode.

Usually the process of memorizing a list of word or figures is more of a left mode activity, with all its weaknesses in terms of performance. The methodology proposed here, which is similar to one used since the 1600s, uses the right mode of the brain instead. In fact, we will use a derived form of The Major System invented by Stanislaus Mink von Wennshein that allows you to build words from any combination of figures. It also permits you to build numbers from any combination of letters.

Would this methodology of memorization work without some reasonable neurological rationale? It is possible, but it would be difficult to persuade you, the reader of this book, to go through it without some reasonable explanation. In short, the method works, regardless of the extent to which future science may eventually determine the exact location and confirm the degree of separation of brain functions in the two hemispheres. New findings on the function of the corpus callosum indicate this huge bundle of nerve fibres connecting the two hemispheres can inhibit the passage of information from hemisphere to hemisphere when a task requires non-interference from one or the other hemisphere. The idea of this process is to inhibit the left part of the brain from capturing information by using a mix of drawings, letters, and figures. This will enable you to use the full power of the massive parallelism of the brain. The pre-format at the hippocampus level with all the boxes will allow us to work in sequential and parallel mode, tricking the system but enhancing the performance. To convert numbers into letters, we will use a specific CODE.

THE CODE

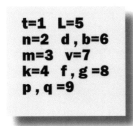

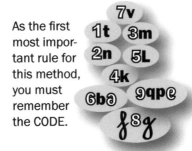

As the first most important rule for this method, you must remember the CODE.

Let's have a closer look at the CODE and see how the reference numbers are given:

t perceived as a drawing, has one leg so it is associated with the number **1**

n has two legs and is associated with the number **2**

m has 3 legs and is associated with the number **3**

K as a drawing is identical to **4**. In addition to that seemingly confusing logic, in some languages k has a phonetic resemblance; for example, 4 = *quattro* in Italian or *quatre* in French, which have a strong k sound.

L will represent the five in fifty, in Roman Numerals

b and **d** are similar in style when drawing the number **6**

v is similar to **7**

f and **g** have the same movement when writing the number **8**

q or **p** is closely associated with the style of number **9**

4

Logically, you may want to dispute some of the CODE'S rationale, but for argument's sake, avoid any desire for debate and simply remember it for now.

In memorizing this CODE, you are opening the doors to an exciting memory opportunity.

In this book all the letters from the CODE are in black, and all the other vowels or letters considered neutral and not belonging to the CODE will be in red.

Let us start with the first ten boxes from 1 to 10. This will be the start of your storage space system. Thereafter we will continue through to number 44 — the objective of this book, which is to know and remember all forty-four presidents of the United States.

AN EXCEPTION TO THE RULE: We must start with an exception, and it will be the only exception to the rule, I assure you. The exceptions are for the numbers 1–10 only. These ten numbers and their rhyming counterparts must be remembered by heart, along with the CODE.

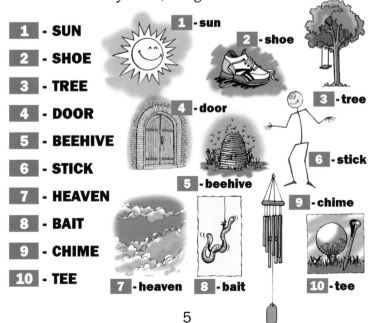

1 - SUN
2 - SHOE
3 - TREE
4 - DOOR
5 - BEEHIVE
6 - STICK
7 - HEAVEN
8 - BAIT
9 - CHIME
10 - TEE

Now comes the amusing part of utilizing both parts of your brain by using the CODE.

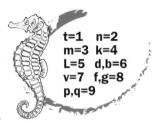

t=1   n=2
m=3   k=4
L=5   d,b=6
v=7   f,g=8
p,q=9

11
toto

11: The word will contain two t's and the letters in between will have to be neutral, meaning not a letter from our CODE. As you noticed, all the letters of the CODE are consonants and any vowels will be neutral.

Remember! As we are starting to work on the word association for the 11th President, we need to use 1 & 1 (for 11), in other words t & t.

The first word that comes to mind is Toto, Judy Garland's dog in The Wizard of Oz. Let us use the code t=1 o=NEUTRAL t=1 o=NEUTRAL; therefore, Toto=11. **toto**.

12
tan

12: The word should contain t and n which equals 1 and 2 in the CODE. Tan comes to mind, with images of a woman sunbathing on the beach. **tan**.

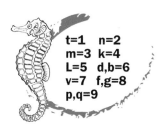

t=1   n=2
m=3   k=4
L=5   d,b=6
v=7   f,g=8
p,q=9

13
tam

13: t and m: Tam as in the Scottish bonnet worn by men, but for my purposes I placed it on a lady. The tam was named after the character Tam O'Shanter in the poem by Robert Burns. **tam**.

14
teck

14: t and k. The exception with teck is that c is not a vowel and is not part of the CODE, so it is neutral too. **teck**.

15
taiL

15: t and l: the tail of the whale. **taiL**.

16
tab

16: t and b: pop topsor pull tab, the tab is the ring that you pull to open a soft drink or beer can. **tab**.

17
tv

17: t and v: An easy association is the TV. **tv**.

18
tag

18: t and g: the world tag, the graffiti, or, more specifically, the signature of graffiti artists. **tag**.

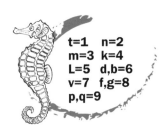

```
t=1   n=2
m=3   k=4
L=5   d,b=6
v=7   f,g=8
p,q=9
```

19
tap

19: t and p: A tap, usually re-stricted to uses such as beer taps and a faucet as water outlets, but there we will use it in the broader sense. **tap**.

20
no

Dr NO

20: n and o: The famous James Bond movie. Dr NO. **no**.

21
net

21: n and t: The net, as in basket-ball net. **net**.

22
nun

22: n and n: Why not a nun? **nun**.

23

nemo

23: n and m: the famous Nemo, the clown fish. nemo.

24
neck

24: n and k: the neck. **neck**.

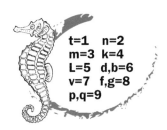

t=1 n=2
m=3 k=4
L=5 d,b=6
v=7 f,g=8
p,q=9

25
niLe

25: n and L: the Nile, with a fishing boat or felucca. **niLe**.

26
noddy

26: n and d: Noddy the famous character created by British children's author Enid Blyton. **noddy**.

27
navy

27: n and v: the Navy. **navy**.

28
nog

28: n and g: Nog, a Star Trek character; the *Deep Space Nine* urchin who became Starfleet's first Ferengi officer, played by Aaron Eisenberg. **nog**.

29
nap

29: n and p: Take a nap in a hammock. **nap**.

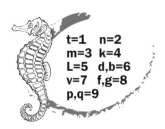

```
t=1   n=2
m=3   k=4
L=5   d,b=6
v=7   f,g=8
p,q=9
```

30
me

30: me: Self-portrait. **me**.

31
mat

31: m and t: as checkmate in a chess game. **mat**.

32
moon

32: m and n: as moon. **moon**

33
mum

33: m and m: as mum. **mum**.

34
moka

34: m and k: as in a good cup of moka coffee. **moka**.

35
moLe

35: m and L: as a mole. **moLe**.

36
mob

36: m and b: as mob, the Godfather and the mob wars. **mob**.

37
movie

37: m and v: as a movie theater. **movie**.

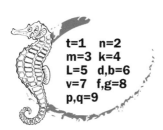

t=1   n=2
m=3   k=4
L=5   d,b=6
v=7   f,g=8
p,q=9

38: m and g: As the famous American mug. **mug** .

38
mug

39: m and p: as a map. **map**

39
map

40: k and o: As KO, a girl who is a knockout. **ko**.

40
ko

41: k and t: As a Kit Kat bar, created by Rowntree Limited of York in England and produced worlwide by Nestlé. **kitkat**.

41
kitkat

42: k and n: As Ken, fictional character and America's most beloved doll from Mattel. **ken**.

42
ken

43: k and m: As Kim Novak, one of America's most popular movie stars in the late 1950s. **kim**.

43
kim

44: k and k: As khaki, coloured material in military uniforms. **khaki**.

44
khaki

11

A simple exercise now is to close your eyes and try to remember the list of the forty-four boxes you just read through.

At this stage, you should be able to picture each number with each drawing because you have memorized the CODE.

1 & 1 (11) = t & t, which in turn is Toto.

1 & 7 (17) = t & v, which in turn is TV.

2 & 3 (23) = n & m, which in turn is Nemo.

Can you still picture the images you saw? If not at this stage, I would recommend that you go back through them again before moving on to the next chapter. It is imperative to memorize the CODE.

The next chapter will build important associations that will tie it all together, giving you a rush as you realize the potential that you now have in your hands.

If you're among those who complain about not having a good memory, then this will soon be a thing of the past.

In fact, it is the way that you capture and process the information that makes the difference. Your brain works just fine—the only issue is you were not trained to process the information properly. Data capture is the problem or, to be more specific, the shift to a particular way of processing visual information.

You may not believe it at this moment. You may have that wonderful trait of scepticism, and I understand that, as I am the biggest sceptic of all. Proof, give me proof! is my motto.

This book is designed to help you make a mental shift and gain a two-fold advantage. Sceptic or not, by the end of this book you will know the forty-four presidents of the United States, both sequentially and randomly.

They say a picture is worth a thousand words. All the visual stimuli are by far richer than a list of words. An image induces a slightly different state of consciousness, especially if you yourself sketch a picture to memorize it (regardless of your artistic ability). That is why the third chapter is dedicated specifically to unleashing your memory. The instructions in this book have been designed particularly for people who think they have a poor memory but who might like to enhance it and perhaps become a walking encyclopaedia of information. The approach of this book is different from others in that the instructions are aimed at unleashing your potential in terms of memorization as you are reading and visualizing.

Already, at this point if you have memorized the CODE, then you have just learned a list of forty-four words. If I asked, what number eleven was on the list, the word toto should come to mind and so forth. We have set the stage, we have programmed your hippocampus from one to forty-four and thanks to the CODE, you are now able to manage it sequentially and randomly. You are now ready for the next and most important stage of the game; you will load each box and its picture with a president's name to establish a link.

Chapter 2

Build your associations with your hippocampus

An intriguing aspect of the remarkable gains most readers achieve is the rapid rate of improvement in memory capacity. So far, this book has been limited to forty-four items relating to the forty-four U.S. presidents. However, the principle is that you simply have no limits once you have the basic knowledge of the method and you know the CODE.

As humans, we have all the tools to acquire a great memory, but old habits to process information interfere with that ability and block it. This book is designed to remove that interference (our left-brain habit) and to unblock your ability.

Why would you want to memorize all forty-four American presidents?

Given America's pre-eminent role in the world, knowing the American presidents is essential for discussion, comparison, debate, and lessons learned.

Now that you have set up your hippocampus in Chapter 1, you can get very creative in terms of association for each of the forty-four boxes. The more inventive and personal you make your memory association, the greater the chance you have to retain it.

The major objective is to find an association between each name of the U.S. presidents and the number/name of each box of your hippocampus. All means are required, even the more tortuous.

At the end of this exercise, you will memorize each picture and associate a number with a president. Again, as stated earlier, what is important is the way that you capture the information, using a mixture of drawings, letters, and numbers rather than words alone. This combination will make your memory powerful.

Let's try it together...

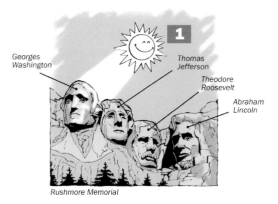

Georges
Washington

Thomas
Jefferson

Theodore
Roosevelt

Abraham
Lincoln

Rushmore Memorial

Association 1: WASHINGTON/SUN/1.

Of course, George Washington was the nation's first president and father of the United States as we know it. Picture the sun rising on the largest work of art on earth: the Mount Rushmore the sun (number 1) and George Washington, and a ray of sunshine stroking the sixty-foot-high face of George Washington. Strong association between the sun (number 1) and George Washington.

Remember, 1 = the rhyming word of SUN

Association 2: ADAMS/SHOE/2.

In the center of the ceiling of the Sistine Chapel are nine scenes from the book of Genesis, of which the creation of Adam is the best known. This time the focus won't be on the hands of God and Adam, with the hand of God giving life to Adam, but instead it is on Adam's foot wearing a tennis shoe, linking President John Adams to the number 2 (shoe).

Remember, 2 = the rhyming word of SHOE

Adam

SHOE

Jefferson Memorial  **TREE**

Association 3: JEFFERSON/TREE/3. The Thomas Jefferson Memorial in Washington, DC, is surrounded by Japanese cherry trees linking one of the American founding fathers to the number 3 (tree).

Remember, 3 = the rhyming word of TREE

Association 4: MADISON/DOOR/4. Madison Square Garden IV at Pennsylvania Station, New York City, is best known as home of the New York Knicks of the NBA and the New York Rangers of the NHL. A big door in the middle links James Madison to the number 4 (door).

Madison Square Garden

4 DOOR

Remember, 4 = the rhyming word of DOOR

BEEHIVE 5

Association 5: MONROE/BEEHIVE/5. Picture Marilyn Monroe as an attractive bee in black and yellow, flying around the beehive.

Remember, 5 = the rhyming word of BEEHIVE

Association 6: QUINCY/ADAM/ MANSTICK/6. John Quincy Adams, the son of the second president. The major challenge is to avoid confusion with the drawing of Adam in Association 2. Instead, focus here on Quincy Jones and a stickman named Adam who is carrying an apple.

Remember, 6 = the rhyming word of MANSTICK

6 STICK

Association 7: JACKSON/ HEAVEN/7. President Andrew Jackson. The King of Pop, Michael Jackson, is floating in the heavens, as seen from the window of a plane.

Remember, 7 = the rhyming word of HEAVEN

7 HEAVEN

Association 8: VAN BUREN/BAIT/8. Martin Van Buren. The name Daniel Buren, a French conceptual artist comes to mind.

It is more commonly referred to as the Colonnes de Buren (Buren's Columns). We picture a murène, a long fish that resembles a snake with Colonnes de Buren (columns of Buren) on it. The murène swallows the bait, linking Van Buren to Number 8 (bait).

8 BAIT

Remember, 8 = the rhyming word of BAIT

Association 9: HARRISON/CHIME/9. Georges Harrison, the famous guitarist of the Beatles. He was known for his interest in Indian music and for playing Aeolian chimes.

Remember, 9 = the rhyming word of CHIME

9 CHIME

10 TEE

Association 10: TYLER/TEE/10

Liv Tyler (actress) starred as the daughter of Bruce Willis in the movie *Armageddon*.

In this 10th association, President John Tyler is represented as Liv Tyler on a golf tee.

Remember, 10 = the rhyming word of TEE

11 toto

Association 11: POLK/TOTO/11. Polk Audio is an award-winning designer and manufacturer of high-performance audio products.

The association is Toto listening to Dorothy singing "Over the Rainbow" on two large Polk loudspeakers.

12
tan

Association 12: TAYLOR/ TAN/12. Robert Taylor, the man with the perfect profile and dashing good looks, on the beach with an attractive suntanned girl.

13 **tam**

Association 13: FILLMORE/TAM/13. Fillmore is the famous hippie VW bus and Radiator Springs' resident in the children's all-time favourite movie, *Cars*. Fillmore is wearing a tam; in fact, a Rastafarian tam (or Rasta tam).).

Association 14: PIERCE/TECK/14. In the movie *After the Sunset*, Pierce Brosnan lounges on the beautiful Teck deck that Salma Hayek built.

14 **teck**

Association 15: BUCHANAN/ TAIL/15. A whale taking a shower in Lake Buchanan under the 3,200-foot canyon waterfalls.

15 taiL

Association 16: LINCOLN/TAB/16. In the Lincoln Memorial, located in the National Mall in Washington, DC, we associate the sculptor Daniel Chester French putting the finishing touches on this famous statue with a can of Coca Cola with the pull-tab opened, ready to drink.

NOTE: Far-fetched associations will help you remember the data much easier.

Abraham Lincoln

Association 17: JOHNSON/TV/7. Magic Johnson, the famous professional basketball player from the Lakers, crashing out of the screen of a TV. Make a link between President Andrew Johnson, initiator of the 13th Amendment that abolished slavery and the number 17 (TV).

Association 18: GRANT/TAG/18. Grant Memorial in Washington, DC, with the equestrian statue of General Grant, the second-largest equestrian statue in the world, tagged, and linking Grant with 18(Tag), according to the CODE.

Carmen Hayes

Association 19: HAYES/TAP/19. The world famous porn-ebony-star Carmen Hayes, taking a shower under a huge tap.

Association 20: GARFIELD/ NO/20. The lazy, selfish, overweight orange tabby cat standing sheepishly next to James Bond in *Dr. No.*

Association 21: ARTHUR/ NET/21. King Arthur in a jousting tournament, a basketball at the top of his lance, attacking a basketball hoop.

Association 22: CLEVELAND/ NUN/22. Related to General Moses Cleveland from whom the city of Cleveland, Ohio, was named. Grover Cleveland was named this way in honor of the first pastor of the First Presbyterian Church of Caldwell where his father was pastor. The nun gives relevance to the church link.

Association 23: HARRISON/ NEMO/23. Benjamin Harrison was the only president hailing from Indiana. Harrison Ford, better known as Indiana Jones, is depicted here grabbing Nemo's tail.

NOTE: Associations do not have to have logical sense but "memorable" meaning.

Association 24: GROVER CLEVE-
LAND/NECK/24. The second campaign of Cleveland against Benjamin
Harrison was a victory by a wide
margin. His victory was head and
shoulders above the rest.

neck

Association 25: MCKINLEY
HAT/NILE/25. After the assassin's
shot. McKinley turned and walked
steadily to a chair and seated himself, simultaneously removing his
hat and bowing his head toward
his hands. We can see McKinley's
hat at the top of the mast of the
sailboat on the Nile.

niLe

Association 26: THEODORE
ROOSEVELT/NODDY/26. Theodore
Roosevelt was the fifth cousin of Frank-
lin Roosevelt. Noddy, climbing on Mount
Rushmore on the face of Theodore
Roosevelt, linking the president to the
number 26 (Noddy).

noddy

Association 27: TAFT/NAVY/27. The Navy in the southern rim of Yosemite Valley at Taft Point, linking between Taft and 27 (Navy).

Association 28: WILSON/Nog and Torrie Wilson/28, one of the World Wrestling Entertainment's most recognized femme fatales, with a tennis ball from the Wilson brand.

Association 29: HARDING/NAP/29. Former Olympic ice skater Tonya Harding, who gained national attention for her involvement in an attack on her chief skating rival Nancy Kerrigan. Skating on the body of a man taking a nap in an hammock, linking Harding to 29 (nap).

Association 30: COOLIDGE/ME/30.
When I think of the name Coolidge in association with Me (30), Jennifer Coolidge
comes to mind as Stiffler's mom in all
three *American Pie* movies.

Jennifer COOLIDGE

Association 31: HOOVER/MAT/31. A
vacuum from the Hoover brand, on a chess-
board, linking Hoover and 31 (Mat).

mat

Association 32: FRANKLIN
ROOSEVELT/MOON/32. Roosevelt
contracted an illness, believed to be
polio (in fact Guillain-Barre syn-
drome), which resulted in his using
a wheelchair in private. As ET makes
Elliott's bike fly in the shadow of the
moon, Roosevelt's wheelchair is doing the same.

moon

33 mum

Association 33: TRUE MAN/ MUM/33. This reflects Truman as the family man and links an image of a young mother holding her baby with Truman proudly standing by her side.

34 moka

Association 34: EISENHOWER/ MOKA/34. Ike with a stove- top coffeemaker. He smoked four packs of cigarettes a day until 1949 and often drank fifteen cups of coffee a day.

35 moLe

Association 35: JFK/MOLE/35. John F. Kennedy's assassination. The media linked it to the possibility of a CIA mole.

Association 36: LYNDON JOHN-SON/MOB/36. Bobby Baker, President Lyndon Johnson's unofficial vice president, whose scandalous activities involved several prominent mob bosses, became the basis for the first major political embarrassment of the Johnson administration.

36
mob

37 movie

Association 37: NIXON/MOVIE/37. The Watergate scandal and its extensive cover-up led to President Richard Nixon's fall from grace. The famous movie, Nixon, directed by Oliver Stone in 1995, featured a controversial Anthony Hopkins as the main character.

Association 38: FORD/MUG/38. This features the Ford Motor Company's brand on a mug.

38
mug

Association 39: JIMMY CARTER/ MAP/39. The famous Jimmy Carter peanut statue in Plains, Georgia, depicted here on a tourist map. By using scientific farming techniques, Carter expanded the family peanut business.

Association 40: REAGAN/KO/40.

Ronald Reagan knocking out the Soviet Union by outspending them on defence.

Association 41: BUSH/KIT/41. Did you know that Bush's father and his mother, Barbara, had a passion for chocolate bars?

Association 42: CLINTON/ KEN/42. This links the resemblance of former President Bill Clinton and the famous Ken doll from Mattel.

Association 43: G.W. BUSH/ KIM/43. Abstinence is a favorite subject of President George W. Bush. The image is the sensual persona of Kim Novak (a famous actress in the late 50s), adding spice to this association.

Association 44: OBAMA/ KHAKI/44

Obama is the 44th president. The fact that khaki is the associative word lends irony to the current political state, which is the right outfit to deal with the numerous wars where the world is involved.

Chapter 3

Unleash your hippocampus

"The main theme to emerge is that there appear to be two modes of thinking, verbal and non-verbal represented rather separately in left and right hemispheres respectively, and that our educational system, as well as science in general, tends to neglect the non-verbal form of intellect. What it 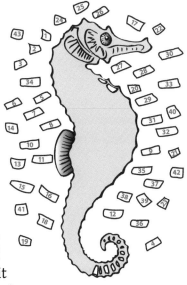 comes down to is that modern so-   c i e t y discriminates against the right hemisphere" (Roger W. Sperry, "Lateral Specialization of Cerebral Function in the Surgically Separated Hemispheres," 1973).

Furthermore, the two modes of processing tend to

interfere with each other, preventing maximum performance. It has been suggested that this might be a rationale for the evolutionary development of asymmetry in the human brain as a means of keeping the two different modes of processing in two different hemispheres. All mnemonics are bridges between the two hemispheres in order to help the two parts work in harmony.

As Betty Edwards explains in her popular book, Drawing on the Right Side of the Brain, unless there is some monkey that we don't know about out there in the forest drawing pictures of other monkeys, we can assume that drawing visual information is an activity confined to human beings and made possible by our human brain. Therefore, it should be of interest in processing information coming to our brains.

The mode of processing used by the right brain is rapid, complex, whole-pattern, spatial, and perceptual. It is this mode that is used in this book.

In order to memorize the forty-four US Presidents, we used a relational interface based on rhyme and visual association in accordance with figures for those in the first ten toolboxes. From numbers 11 to 44 we used a visual linking of figures to letters only.

Half a brain is better than no brain, but a whole brain is better than a half!

Now, someone (a right-brainer), might say, "What is the interest in knowing all presidents sequentially by their number of appearance in the White House?" The answer is that we are living in a world driven by left-brainers, and they crave to acquire this kind of analytical, sequential, abstract, and rational kind of power, but they can't get it easily or quickly without the help of the right side of the brain.

You will be able to demonstrate your memorization skills if you want to dazzle the crowd during a dinner party. Left-brainers (meaning the majority) will be amazed by your apparent intellect. Right-brainers (mostly artists) will see you as a nerd or geek, a kind of Rain Man. Everyone, however, will have to admit that your knowledge is clear, correct, and quickly retrievable.

One main problem is that the left brain is dominant, speedy, and prone to hurrying, so the idea is to find a way to turn down the task by the dominant left brain...

Everyone knows the old "Who's on First?" routine from Abbott and Costello. At this stage, you should be able to create a new routine because you have learned the fundamentals.

Who's on fifteen? Answer: the number 15 is t + L, or taiL, which is associated with a whale taking a shower in Lake Buchanan, so Buchanan is the 15th U.S. president, etc.

Try it—you will be amazed. You will know by heart all forty-four American presidents; you will know them randomly—and vice versa. If you know the name, you can find the ranking!

You can reach higher levels with a little bit of homework. Take your pen and find information for each president. In the annex you will find a left-brain summary with the main events for each president; simply translate this information through a mind map. (All techniques using different drawings from Tony Buzzan are well known and accessible on the web).

Below is an example the first president, George Washington.

You will see that you can load additional information very easily, and your memory can store a lot of data under this format.

Each president's figure is prepared, and you can use this book to do your homework. All are in a chronological order to help you to add new information and to memorize them easily. By the way, you probably noticed already that you did not need to know their ranking anymore. Enjoy!

1789 - 1797
(2 TERMS)

Georges WASHINGTON

Unleash your right brain.

- Was born into a well-to-do Virginia Planter family
- In October 1781, with the aid of French allies, Washington forced the British to surrender at Yorktown, Virginia
- President from 1789 to 1797
- Decided on neutrality during the war between France and England in 1793
- The only president inaugurated in two cities: New York and Philadelphia
- Wore false teeth made from exotic materials
- Within three years of leaving office, died at his home at Mount Vernon, Virginia, on December 14, 1799, at the age of 67

Georges
WASHINGTON 1

1
SUN

John
ADAMS 2

2
SHOE

Adam

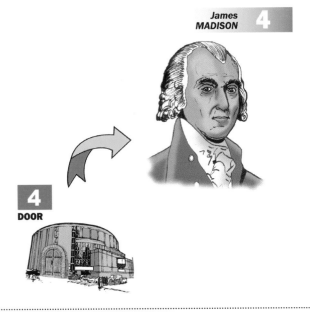

James MONROE **5**

5 BEEHIVE

John Quicy ADAMS **6**

6 STICKS

Andrew JOHNSON 7

7 **HEAVEN**

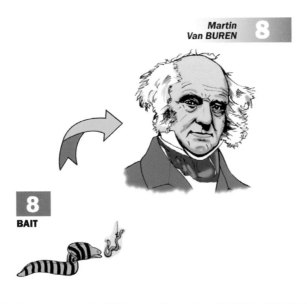

Martin Van BUREN 8

8 **BAIT**

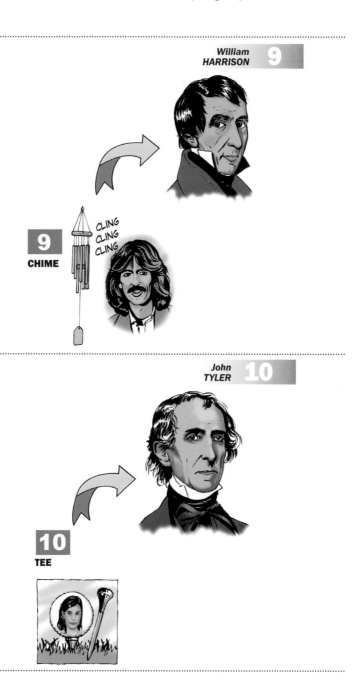

James K. POLK 11

11 toto

Zacharie TAYLOR 12

12 tan

Robert TAYLOR

Millard
FILLMORE 13

13
tam

Franklin
PIERCE 14

14
teck

James
BUCHANAN **15**

15
taiL

Abraham
LINCOLN **16**

16
tab

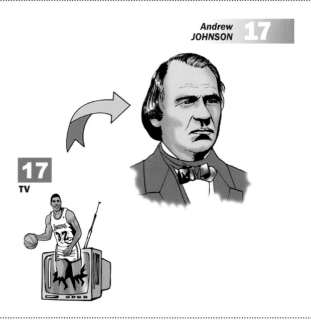

Andrew JOHNSON 17

17 TV

Ulysse GRANT 18

18 tag

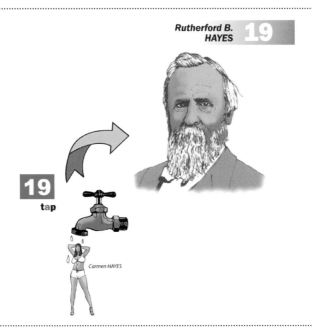

Rutherford B. **HAYES** **19**

19 tap

Carmen HAYES

James **GARFIELD** **20**

20 no

Chester
ARTHUR 21

21
net

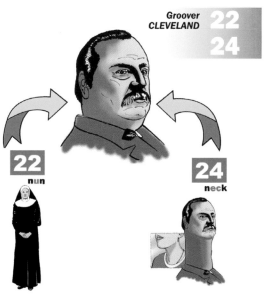

Groover
CLEVELAND 22
24

22
nun

24
neck

Benjamin
HARRISON 23

23
nemo

William
MAC KINLEY 25

25
niLe

49

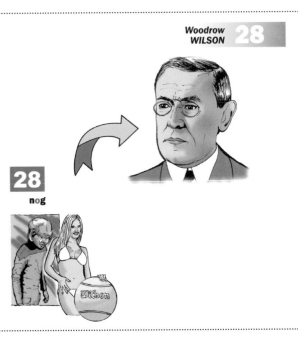

Woodrow **WILSON** **28**

28
nog

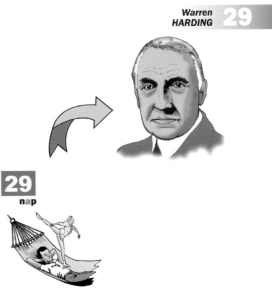

Warren **HARDING** **29**

29
nap

Calvin
COOLIDGE **30**

30
me

Jennifer COOLIDGE

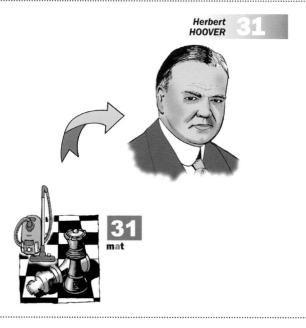

Herbert
HOOVER **31**

31
mat

Franklin Delanoe
ROOSEVELT 32

32 moon

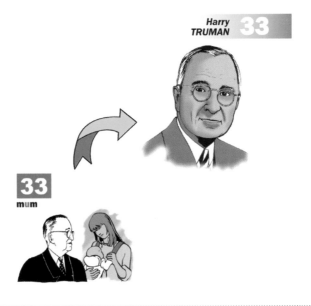

Harry
TRUMAN 33

33 mum

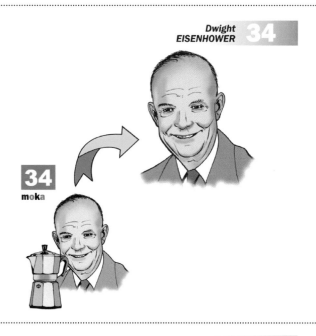

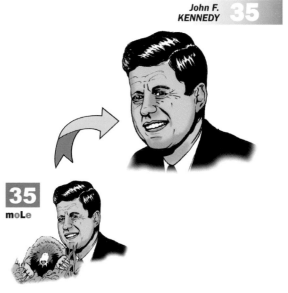

53

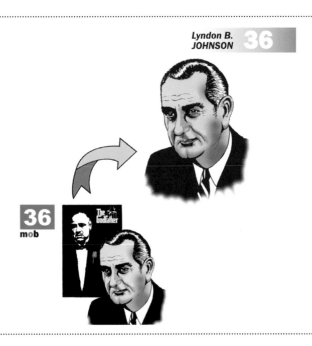

Lyndon B. JOHNSON 36

36 mob

Richard NIXON 37

37 movie

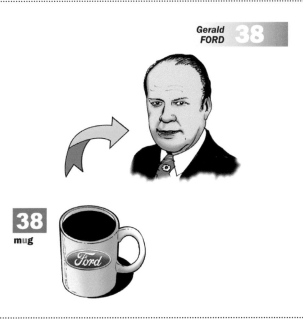

Gerald FORD 38

38 mug

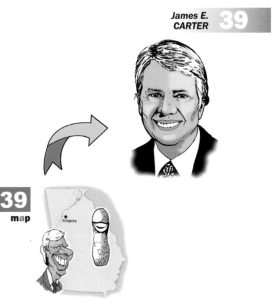

James E. CARTER 39

39 map

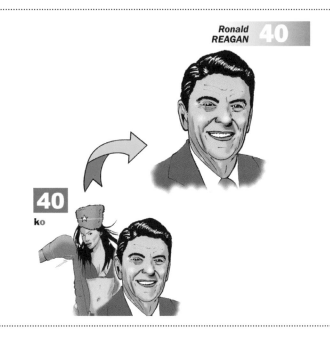

Ronald
REAGAN **40**

40
ko

Georges
BUSH **41**

41
kitkat

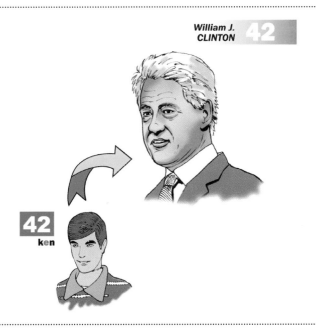

William J. CLINTON 42

42 ken

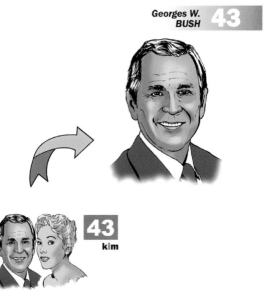

Georges W. BUSH 43

43 kim

Conclusion

The example here, of memorizing all forty-four U.S. presidents is only one aspect involved in the acquisition and storage of data in our brains. Beyond this, the possibilities to build your own system and to set up your own hippocampus are endless. The rapid and holistic right brain and the slow, analytical left brain will work well together. Thanks to the CODE in this book, we can change the environment and let the two sides of our brains work together, bridging one with the other through the corpus callosum.

In Chapter 3, you were confronted with your ability to draw and translate your own information in order to process data with your right brain and use your capacity and rapidity. Everyone knows how to draw, which is a major strength of each human being (unless some monkeys somewhere are drawing pictures).

I am sure that you have become amazed by the quantity of additional and pertinent information you can memorize this way. Ultimately, the more you progress in your ability to memorize, the more you increase your self-confidence. Whether you have forty-four or even thousands of items to memorize, everything becomes possible.

In case you want to increase your number of boxes in your hippocampus, you can write directly to dr_johnnyfrog@yahoo.com to get your tool kit for 50-100-200 etc until 1,000 boxes.

You can also submit any idea for book to memorize long serial of names associated to a ranking and become a co-author of this book.

By understanding and applying these techniques, you can change the concept of the personal computer by building your own personal computer—without needing a battery, special software, or applications. You can now be successful in decreasing your entropy by increasing the flow of information you can store. We can evolve from Homo sapiens to Homo entropicus. Let us play with the plasticity of our brain; let us create this new human species.

In the meantime, you will never again have to ask yourself "Who's on first?" or "What's on second?" You will know that numbers twenty-two and twenty-four have the same name because they are the same person. You will know that numbers nine and twenty-three had the same last name, but the latter was the former's grandson. You will know that numbers seventeen and thirty-six shared the same surname but without any family connection, whereas twenty-six and thirty-two also shared the same surname but were cousins. You will know that numbers forty-one and forty-three were father and son, as were six and two. We know by now that the forty-fourth U.S. president is Barack Obama. If re-elected in four years he will be still the forty-fourth , if not the key question will remain: Who will be the forty-fifth?

Annex

(from *The New Big Book of US Presidents* by Marc Frey and Todd Davis)

George Washington
- The only president inaugurated in two cities: New York and Philadelphia
- Wore false teeth made from exotic material
- With the aid of French allies, forced the British to surrender at Yorktown, Virginia
- Was born into a well-to-do Virginia planter family
- 1789-1797

John Adams
- The first president to live in the White House
- As a lawyer in Boston, he successfully defended British soldiers accused in the Boston massacre
- Federalist 1797-1801
- Died July 4th at age 91 on the 50th anniversary of the Declaration of Independence

Thomas Jefferson
- Played the violin
- His library of 6,000 books was the basis for the Library of Congress

- Died on July 4th, 1826, just hours before the death of his great friend and rival John Adams
- Democratic Republican, 1801-1809

James Madison
- Stood 5'4" and weighed about 100 pounds
- Died in 1836, the last of the founding fathers
- Democratic Republican, 1809-1817

James Monroe
- Received all but one electoral vote in the 1820 election
- Left the White House in debt
- Died July 4th as did Adams and Jefferson
- Democratic Republican, 1817-1825

John Quincy Adams
- Inaugurated when all the former presidents, except for Washington, were still alive
- His wife was pregnant nineteen times in twenty-two years
- Democratic Republican, 1825-1829

Andrew Jackson
- Survived his first assassination attempt
- Killed a man in duel
- Earned the nickname "Old Hickory" for being as tough as wood
- Named "King Andy" by the Whig Party
- Democrat, 1829-1837

Martin Van Buren
- The first president born as a U.S. citizen
- The eighth president, he lived to see the election of eight different presidents from eight different states
- Democrat, 1837-1841

William Henry Harrison
- The first candidate to have a campaign slogan, "Tippecanoe and Tyler too," disguising his aristocratic background, advertising himself as a common frontiersman, and a self-made man.
- First president of the Whig party
- Gave the longest inauguration speech of any president (8,445 words)
- His grandson, Benjamin, became president forty-eight years later.
- Whig, March-April 1841

John Tyler
- First president to remarry after being widowed
- Only president to serve in both the United States and Confederate governments
- First vice president elevated to the presidency due to the chief executive's death
- Whig, 1841-1845

James K. Polk
- Only president to have been Speaker of the House of Representatives
- Acquired the most land for the United States since the Louisiana Purchase: California, Nevada, Arizona, Utah, and New Mexico
- Democrat, 1845-1849

Zachary Taylor
- First president not previously elected to any other public office
- Famous for his sloppy appearance
- Nicknamed "Old Rough and Ready" because of his simple and direct manner
- Whig, 1849-1850

Millard Fillmore
- His wife established the White House library
- -In retirement, he served as President of the Buffalo Historical Society
- Whig, 1850-1853

Franklin Pierce
- All three of his children died during childhood
- First president to memorize his inaugural address
- Democrat, 1853-1857

James Buchanan
- The only president never to marry
- Because of the Civil War, Buchanan believed he would be the last president
- Democrat, 1857-1861

Abraham Lincoln
- First president born outside the original thirteen colonies
- At 6'4", the tallest president
- On April 14, 1865, John Wilkes Booth, a southern sympathizer, assassinated him and he died the following day
- Republican, 1861-1865

Andrew Johnson
- He was seventeen before he learned to read
- The only former president elected to the U.S. Senate
- Democrat, 1865-1869

Ulysses S. Grant
- Mark Twain helped him publish his memoirs
- Received a speeding ticket on his horse
- Republican, 1869-1877

Rutherford B. Hayes
- Won several spelling contests as a child
- His wife was the first First Lady to graduate from college (Wesleyan)
- Republican, 1877-1881

James A. Garfield
- Last president born in a log cabin
- Wrote in both Latin and Greek
- Was president less than eight months
- Republican, 1881

Chester A. Arthur
- Called "Elegant Arthur" for his fashionable clothes
- Passionately protected his private life from the press
- Republican, 1881-1885

Grover Cleveland
- The Baby Ruth candy bar was named after his daughter, Ruth
- Paid someone to fight for him during the Civil War
- Democrat, 1885-1889; 1893-1897

Benjamin Harrison
- First president with electricity in the White House
- Called the "Pious Moonlight Dude" for his romantic ways
- Republican, 1889-1893

William McKinley
- His wife had epileptic seizures
- Told guards not to harm his assassin
- Leon Czolgosz, anarchist, shot him in Buffalo, New York
- Died days later, becoming America's third president to be assassinated
- Republican, 1897-1901

Theodore Roosevelt
- Teddy bears were named after him
- By visiting Panama in 1906, he became the first president to leave the continental United States
- Republican, 1901-1909

William Howard Taft
- First president to throw the ceremonial first pitch of the baseball season
- First president to have a presidential vehicle
- Republican, 1909-1913

Woodrow Wilson
- Only president to have a PhD
- Only president buried in Washington, DC
- Democrat, 1913-1921

Warren G. Harding
- First president to visit Alaska
- First president to ride in a car at his inauguration
- Republican, 1921-1923

Calvin Coolidge
- His father swore him in as president
- One of three majors to become president
- Republican, 1923-1928

Herbert Hoover
- First president born west of the Mississippi River
- Refused to accept a salary for the presidency
- Republican, 1929-1933

Franklin D. Roosevelt
- Appointed the first woman, Frances Perkins, to the cabinet
- Was the only disabled president
- Democrat, 1933-1945

Harry S. Truman
- His wife was the longest-living First lady
- Played piano to relax
- Democrat, 1945-1953

Dwight D. Eisenhower
- His favorite books were the westerns of Zane Grey
- Considered working as a cowboy in Argentina
- Republican, 1953-1961

John F. Kennedy
- His favorite meal was tomato soup with sour cream
- Appointed his brother, Robert, as Attorney General
- Was assassinated by Lee Harvey Oswald in Dallas, Texas
- Democrat, 1961-1963

Lyndon B. Johnson
- Obsessively watched the evening news on multiple televisions
- Enjoyed high-speed drives around his Texas ranch
- Democrat, 1963-1969

Richard M. Nixon
- The first president to have visited all fifty states
- Suffered from insomnia during his presidency
- Was implicated in the Watergate Crisis
- Republican, 1969-1974

Gerald R. Ford
- Teased by comedians because of his famous clumsiness
- Had the Marine Corps Band play the University of Michigan's fight song instead of "Hail to the Chief"
- Republican, 1974-1977

James E. Carter
- Studied nuclear physics while at the Naval Academy
- First elected president since 1932 not to win a second time
- Democrat, 1977-1981

Ronald Reagan
- At sixty-nine, the oldest person ever elected president
- Submitted the first trillion-dollar budget to Congress
- Republican, 1981-1989

George Bush
- First incumbent vice president elected since Martin Van Buren
- First president to have been Director of the CIA
- Republican, 1989-1993

William J. Clinton
- Plays the saxophone
- In 1969, he integrated a whites-only swimming pool in Hot Springs, Arkansas
- Democrat, 1993-2001

George W. Bush
- Was elected amid uncertainty after losing the popular vote but benefited from an abbreviated vote count in Florida
- Made retired General Colin Powell the first African-American Secretary of State
- Republican, 2001-2009

Barack Obama (Work in Progress)

LaVergne, TN USA
29 March 2010
1746LVUK00001B